Home Team
Poems About Baseball

Home Team
Poems About Baseball

Edwin Romond

GRAYSON BOOKS
West Hartford, CT
graysonbooks.com

Published by Grayson Books
West Hartford, CT

ISBN: 978-0-9994327-3-0

Book Design: Cindy Mercier
Cover Photo: © Garry Gay, garry-gay.pixels.com

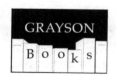

for
Don Colburn

Acknowledgments

Grateful acknowledgement is made to the journals and books in which the following poems, some in slightly different versions, previously appeared:

Aethlon: The Journal of American Sports Literature "A Friend Sends Me Old Baseball Cards in a Book of Poetry," "Loving the Distant Men"

Exit 13, "At the Mazeroski Wall," "Old Yankee Stadium Seat"

Fan Magazine, "Pitchers and Catchers"

New Letters, "Celebrity Signing at a Baseball Card Show"

Spitball, "At Fenway," "Dravecky Dreams," "Meeting Joe Black"

The Sun, "Home Team," "Something I Could Tell You about Love"

"Something I Could Tell You about Love" was reprinted in *Line Drives: 100 Contemporary Baseball Poems*, University of Southern Illinois Press.

Contents

Home Team, 1959

First base sidled the front of Cinkota's Bar
where Hungarian refugees lifted Rheingold
to toast the life of immigrants till shouts

moved them to stagger down the steps, noses red
as sponge balls, and watch our strange game
where home was a hint of white in the early dark.

They'd mill about, drinking and pointing,
then one would ask, "Please, yes?" and we'd nod
and make room for foreigners loving our American

game that they played with the grace of maniacs.
Their baggy black pants and white shirts flapped
like flags as they stomped Albert Street chasing

fly balls that hid in the maze of wires waiting
to dive through cupped hands, sting their noses
and skip among the wheels of Mr. Toth's DeSoto.

Later they'd buy us bottles of Coke that chilled
our hands in the air of August and, as we grieved
the clench of next month's teachers, they rejoiced,

like winners. These men, who had fled the Red death
of Budapest, made it home with us on Albert Street
where we opened arms and cried, "Safe! You're safe!"

The Last Day of My Childhood

The first four innings Buzzy smacked two homers
that jiggled the towels on Petros' clothesline.
It was my $2 hardball so I had to endure Mrs. Petro
who stooped screeching through her kitchen window
that I would "get it" if I bothered her wash again.

But Buzzy was hot that steamy August morning
and leaned into a fastball that climbed the sky
and landed again in the sway of Petros' laundry.
Both teams threw gloves into bike baskets and took off
down the Woodbridge streets, hysterical at leaving me

to crawl like a dog through the walls of clothes.
Mrs. Petro screamed that she was dialing my father
as I raced around the yard until a hand touched me
between the sheets. It belonged to her daughter,
Kathy Ann, one year younger, an 8th grader next week.

She grinned and held my ball like Eve offering an apple,
her eyes flashed green and wicked as she squeezed it
into my hand before guiding me through a maze
of bedspreads and pillow cases. "This way!"
she whispered beneath the shrieks of her mom

and suddenly I was safe on the sidewalk, looking back
to watch her wiggle in cut-offs through the side door.
I pedaled home past the old State Theater.
Godzilla was playing that Saturday night
and I stopped to buy tickets for two.

A Friend Sends Me Old Baseball Cards in a Book of Poetry

In the 50's they stuck to flat bubblegum
but today I open a gift book of poems
and they float like butterflies into my lap.
The book speaks the somber stuff of living
and dying, all its lines broken

from cover to cover. But these faces grin
forever young from mounds and dugouts,
their faces bright with the life of baseball.
So I prop them on my shelves
against the hardbacks of literature

and consider how half these men have died,
the rest live gray and chunky into their 80's,
maybe grieving the game that faded
to lunatic contracts and plastic grass.
I love how they grin from my tiers of books;

I love how I feel as I smile back.

Something I Could Tell You about Love

The soft smack of pitches from my father
who's never cared for baseball, and never asks
about my Yankees. He doesn't want a glove,
just lets my hardball disappear into his hands
already sore from steering his truck without AC
or radio through the decay of Newark and Elizabeth.
My father, whose shirt's glued with sweat,
knows drums and crates must be loaded tonight
but still he stands and throws to me across the hood
of his '53 Ford sagging with freight he'll have to carry
tomorrow into hardware stores and dentists' offices.
Tonight I pound the Rawlings glove he bought me
and watch his face grow dim in the dark of our yard,
then the white ball from his hands into the August heat.
I'm playing catch with my father, who's never liked baseball,
who nods when I ask for five minutes more.

God Gives Faith to Baseball Fans

Remember those first mornings out of school,
the long, lush hours on fields of green
where you first learned that true friendship
can thrive in conflict and the music

of chatter and cheers could bloom into symphony?
There will be no slide into the empty innings
of middle aged softball with its sloppy
beer keg games, where bellies bulge tee shirts

and no one keeps track of the score. No,
I, who gave you time and love beyond time,
vow with a rainbow more of this splendor
when the life you know ends and the rapture

of endlessness begins. There'll be Padres playing
and, of course, Angels, but no night games,
no domes, and no one dressed as a chicken.
Bring your spikes—the grass will be real.

Loving the Distant Men

for Thurman Munson

First, I loved you on the TV screen,
how you'd rage like a pinched bear
when you muffed one but more for the calm
that filled your eyes when you'd waddle
out to soothe a rattled southpaw.
And some jeered that you looked like a walrus
but, to me, you were splendid barreling home
with the wild joy of winning for strangers
who needed you from each seat in the ball park.

And I was there that October afternoon
when you squinted in the ninth inning glare
then smashed a fastball deep into the bleachers
and made us all feel like champions.
Long after they cleared the field we stayed
to scream your name, begging you back
for one last bow till finally you leaped
from the dugout and swung your cap high
as we rocked the stands with thunder.
Then, as you danced around and around
in the dying sunlight, you opened your arms
wide, as if you longed to hold us all
against your muddy pinstripes.

And far away in the upper deck I watched you
and felt an old joy from summer nights
when I was a kid who stood at railings waving
at the burly truck drivers. Those hulking men
in semis would smile up and yank their horns
before fading into the fumes of the turnpike.
How I yearned for those blasts of friendship,
the bonding music from the distant men
who, like you, reached out for a moment
and then barreled on home.

Getting It Right

for Larry Steward

I've heard no one thank him
for guarding the gold
of honor and accuracy
upon an emerald diamond

where whatever choice he makes
riles half the fans behind him.
May this poem then be overdue
applause for the lonely umpire

crouching in early April drizzle
through summer's last heat,
judging play after play, pitch
after pitch, and having the guts

to call them as he sees them.

The High School Faculty Softball Coach Takes Me Aside After the First Game

Listen up,
we know how busy
you must be with writing
and reading or whatever
English teachers do and
we already have
a right fielder
if his pacemaker holds out
so it's okay with us
if you don't make
every single game
because there must be
something else
you'd rather do than sit
with the Gatorade.
But don't get us wrong!
We're glad you're on
our team and, anybody
could have lost four balls
in the sun and, hey, when
we laughed it wasn't
at you, it's just
that someone told a joke
about a jackass
in a jockstrap and
we happened to look
in your direction.

Photograph of Babe, June 13, 1948

He's suited up for nothing more
than using his bat for balance
and, though his back's to the lens,
you know he's looking out to right field,
searching for '27 and counting to 60.
Like time, the camera caught Babe
from behind—one flash and it was over.
He'll carry #3 no farther than today.

Only One

for Rocky Colavito

I tried to squeeze my Little League bat
across my back as you did, then aim it
like a rifle straight out at the pitcher, but
I still could not hit home runs like you.

I'd measure distance on my street
with the phone poles and could never throw
a ball beyond two but I imagined your throws
sizzling all the way down to the end of Albert St.

In 1959 how I wished I could hit like you
and throw like you, and look cool like you.
But there was only one Rocky Colavito.
Now I stand in the 21st century where Cleveland's

Municipal Stadium used to be and I close my eyes
to see you striding to the plate amidst roars
of love from the stands. I find myself whispering,
 "C'mon, Rocky, get a hold of a fastball and,

for one night only, let's both be young again."

Pitchers and Catchers

for John Fenimore

My pal John stops to borrow
a set of *The Sun Also Rises*.
I count them into his arms
then whisper, as if we're brothers,
"Pitchers and catchers on Friday"
and his grin assures me he can hear
the smack of sliders into stiff mitts.
At lunch the principal stops scolding
a boy for throwing a meatball
and reminds me, "Friday, pitchers
and catchers," and I see rookies
in uniforms numbered three times
their ages next to nervous non-roster
vets who wind up and hope
their new knucklers will be enough.

But here the windows frame only
empty trees and mounds of black snow
and I wish I didn't have to teach
"To Build a Fire" when I'm yearning
for sunny fields in Lauderdale
and Tampa, warm with baseball
chatter and the necessary dreams
of being better than before.
I'll read the sports page this Friday
for the first time since October
and pass these ice days tossing
the words "pitchers and catchers"
to friends who are old enough
to know and young enough to believe

that winter again would come to this.

Going the Distance

for John Halmi

*Robin Roberts pitched 305 complete games
in his Hall of Fame career. —Baseball Reference. com*

Before pitch counts infected baseball
and the term "closer" named a guy
who'd pitch an inning, maybe two,
there were men like Robin Roberts
who finished what they started.
305 times he was the last man standing

on the mound in Connie Mack Stadium.
On boiling summer Sundays or shivering
September nights you could count
on Robin to fire the first pitch
and still be there to throw the last one.

You can't help but tip your cap
to one who worked so hard, staring in
at the batter instead of looking out
to the bullpen for relief. The most
he ever earned was forty thousand,

a raindrop in today's salary tsunamis,
but Robin played for more than money,
something called pride, that passion
to throw as long as he possibly could.
I see him now in heaven pitching

inning after inning after inning
till St. Peter yells, "Hey, Robin,
take a break, eternity's a long time!"
But Roberts just grins and shouts back,
"Relax, Skip, I'm just getting started."

Old Yankee Stadium Seat

for Jeff Febbo

Who knows? This might be the seat
I sat in the night Nettles hit one
to beat the Red Sox, or maybe
the one I splashed tears upon
at the memorial for Thurman in '79.
I do know this seat has seen a lot
of baseball, heard years of cheers
and now, in my friend's home office,
is beautiful as joy in Yankee blue.
I touch it and imagine afternoons
of fathers and mothers with children
or grown men with buddies and beer
feeling friendship in summer air. This
seat locks a history of Yankee baseball,
a fan's consolation in a world of change.
So let your hands hold it like a relic,
close your eyes, and deep in your soul
hear immortal Bob Shepherd
say, *Good afternoon, ladies and*
gentlemen, welcome to Yankee Stadium.
And now, the starting line-ups...

Dravecky Dreams

Dave Dravecky was a San Francisco Giants All-Star pitcher who lost his arm to cancer.

The circle of his arms
broken around his wife,
he has never slept closer
to the mattress, never
sunk deeper into night
as he dreams
his arm's somewhere
waiting like the good news
of a home run hit
after time had been called;
the relief of the umpire
waving the number
off the scoreboard,
the two-handed cheering
from the dugout, the grin
on his catcher signing
a different pitch
and he nodding, winding up,
and feeling what it feels
like to turn back time
and pitch again.

At the Mazeroski Wall
PNC Bank Park, Pittsburgh, PA
for John Cosgrove

It gives me the creeps, this red brick wall
with its faded *406*. I could have my picture
taken in front of it but, for a Yankee fan,
it'd be tasteless as posing with a tomb stone.

The plaque says, *October 13, 1960*, the day I ran
all the way home from 6th grade for the last minutes
of the 7th game of the Yankee–Pirates World Series.
I kept yelling, "Come on! Come on!" at our old TV,

begging it to warm up till finally Ralph Terry
emerged in black and white, getting the sign,
winding up and hurling his fastball to
Bill Mazeroski, who smacked it out to left field.

Yogi looked as if he would catch it, but then
it sailed over his head, over the wall that stands
right in front of me 50 years later. How crushing
at age 11 to lose the World Series and

part of my heart still aches to see that wall up close
and remember Yogi in front of it helpless
as that little squirt Mazeroski danced around
the bases and Pittsburgh started to party

like pirates with rum and trunks of stolen gold.

Baseball in the Dark

for Mel Allen

My radio dial glowed like an August moon as his voice
behind the light took me to such distant cities as Detroit,
Boston, or Chicago. He'd tell me the game like a story

and, at night, with our hall fan buzzing, he made baseball
the story of my life letting me believe the world was filled
with good men like Moose Skowron. Games would last

past eleven and, as my family slept, it'd be just Mel and me,
linked by the wonder of radio that painted each pitch
on the canvas of his voice. When CBS fired him

in '64, it seemed the end of something necessary as faith
in what can't be seen. I used to wish, years later, that luck
might sometime seat us together on an overnight flight

giving me hour after hour to ask about Casey's Yankees.
I'd dream that he'd turn off the overhead light and
it would be Mel again telling me baseball in the dark,

his eyes closed, his summer voice going, going, on and on.

Meeting Joe Black

His face looked fuller than on his baseball card but,
there he was as advertised, Joe Black, ex-Brooklyn Dodger,
out of baseball three years, in Perth Amboy, NJ,
his semi-pro "All-Stars" to play the "Mead St. Aces."

I was 10, had never seen a big-league game in person,
and Joe Black, who had pitched at Ebbetts Field,
was right in front of me in tiny Waters Stadium
older and chunkier than in his Dodger days yet

when he wound up and hurled his first pitch, the ball
looked like an aspirin blazing toward the Mead St. Ace
who didn't stand a chance against a man who used to
strike out Willie Mays at the Polo Grounds.

I had never seen such fastballs and sliders
smacking a catcher's mitt the way Joe Black's did
blurring across the plate to helpless factory workers,
fire fighters, and mechanics in Mead St. Aces uniforms.

He pitched six innings, his faded Dodger jersey darkening
with sweat, and I kept thinking this man had actually pitched
to Stan Musial, to Hank Aaron, to Ernie Banks and, in the '52
Series at Yankee Stadium, to Mickey Mantle.

At the end of the sixth he jogged to the water fountain
near my side of the field and somehow I found the nerve
to stand there as he drank and blurt out, "Hi, Mr. Black."
He turned around, grinned, and said, "Hi, Son,

what's your name?" When I answered, "Edwin,"
he spoke the greatest words I'd ever heard: "I think 'Edwin'
is a very nice name." Then he offered his pitching hand to me
and I shook it feeling his huge fastball fingers squeeze mine

as I entered a *Twilight Zone* moment mentally turning pages
of my Dodger yearbooks where Joe Black was shaking hands
with Roy Campanella, and Gil Hodges, and Jackie Robinson,
and the next morning I would be broadcasting to the world

of St. James School that Joe Black had shaken hands with me.

At Fenway

for Don Colburn

We carry our childhood through
the turnstiles and I lose my breath
in the green arms of Fenway Park.
You and I, friends, graying
into our 50's, finally here
in the steam of this August night.
But I feel like a McCoy at a Hatfield
picnic so even when O'Neill
and El Duque jog right in front of us
I keep my mouth shut and remember
instead games that graced
the old earth of this urban park.
I even give thanks for the Monster
in left, a constant reliable
as friendship, beautiful tonight
beneath the moon and CITGO sign.
But as your guest I don't
confess I see Bucky's ball
climbing October air in '78
and Thurman, one year to live,
hugging him at home plate.
You feel the ghosts here, players
and fans who gathered in summers
gone now to whatever's left
after the final out. Red Sox fans
know about loss and I love them
for that. Strange for a Yankee
fan to think of love at Fenway
but tonight my heart has room
for everyone, especially you,
my baseball brother,
with a red "B" on your cap and
a martyr's faith in your soul, when
your team takes this sacred field
to play our game again.

Celebrity Signing at a Baseball Card Show

The plaster face and greased-back hair
make him look like Bela Lugosi at the end,
dragging Dracula across small town stages,
his life shrinking to the living dead.

We must pay $20 for his name
on a photo of him young and grinning.
His bat's cocked high, his eyes sure
that homers waited in his muscled arms

wet with sweat from a 60's summer
when most of these men were young
as their sons who shift from foot to foot
and ask again what team he played for.

We inch closer to the card table,
and I feel nervous at meeting the one
whose name was atop *The Sporting News*
through two good seasons before trades

to Washington and Cleveland where he played
to empty upper decks, then disappeared
in the necrology of unconditional releases.
I have lived thirty years since his last swing

but still I shake when I hand him the glossy
that he signs so fast his name turns to bubbles
across his uniform. I offer to shake hands
but he grabs his picture from the next in line

who stutters asking about Mickey and '61.
He doesn't answer, just crouches
before us and smears his name
for a ten and two five's.

Blue Mountain Time

In Memory of Bill Zanette

It was luscious gold the sun gave
the outfield grass those years ago
when young men played for love
in the shadows of slate and mountains.
People would come on Sundays, after
dinner on weeknights to sit in the peace
of summer, skipping the radio Phillies'
games for baseball right before their eyes.

And they say Zanette could hit them as far
as dreams could go. How they cheered
when he'd step into a fastball with a blur
of Louisville timber to send it skyward!
And the smells of birch beer and cigar smoke
filled the air loud with love from the bleachers
after he'd hit one in the gloried time
of 50's Blue Mountain League baseball.

Righty or southpaw, change-up,
or curve didn't matter to Zanette
who answered with power anything
offered and pity the fielders with nothing
but hope and leather between them
and the sizzle of line drives from his arms.
And they still remember the young man
with the big heart and ferocious swing

who played each inning as if it were the 9th,
who made pitchers sweat and pray
when he'd step to the plate and stare out
like a lion who's decided it's time for supper.
You'll find his name in the Hall of Fame
and on the lips of my four-year-old son
who already loves the summer game
of his Pappy, the Hall-of-Famer. And some nights

in the dimming yellow dusk I see Zanette
tossing Wiffle ball pitches to my boy
who swings his plastic bat the way
his Pappy's shown him and whacks the ball
all the way to our neighbor's yard.
And, as he circles imaginary bases,
I cheer like a fan, like a father, and
Zanette knows these Blue Mountains
have heard that sound before.

That Night on a Bridge

for Gil Hodges

Forget your homers
and Ebbetts Field cheers
from fans who knew
a saint when they saw one.
You can even forget
your World Series ring and
ticker tape parade through Flatbush.
Just remember that night
on a bridge in Washington
with pitcher Ryne Duren,
staring through his Coke bottle
glasses into the water below and
deciding suicide was the answer
to alcoholism. Think of that night
with Ryne Duren when
his fastball wasn't fast
anymore, the night he clung
to the top of the bridge, drunk
in the darkness, alone
and giving up. Gil, who cares
that you never made it
to the Hall of Fame? So what
if the Dodgers never
retired your number?
We love you for that night
on the bridge when you talked
Ryne Duren down from the railing
then held his life in your arms
as angels cheered from the upper deck
of baseball's summer sky.

Lou Gehrig Day
Yankee Stadium, July 4, 1939
for BJ Ward

He was scared and did not
want to speak to 62,000 people.

Maybe he felt facing death
was enough to endure but

they kept calling his name
till he stepped up to the mic

and gave 278 words of thank you
and goodbye. His body trembled

as he spoke with the voice
of a dying man still strong enough

to unlock his heart before thousands
and let them all come in.

About the Author

Edwin Romond's most recent book is *Alone with Love Songs* (Grayson Books, 2011). His poems have appeared in journals such as *The Sun, Lips, Exit 13, The San Pedro Review, Connecticut River Review, Tiferet, New Letters, Poet Lore, Edison Literary Review, Spitball Magazine, The Stillwater Review, The Journal of New Jersey Poets* as well as in college texts and anthologies. His work has twice been featured on NPR and he received the 2013 New Jersey Poetry Prize for his poem, "Champion." He has been awarded poetry fellowships from the National Endowment for the Arts and from both the New Jersey and Pennsylvania State Councils on the Arts.

Romond was a public school teacher for 32 years in Wisconsin and New Jersey before retiring. He now works part-time in the poetry program of the Geraldine R. Dodge Foundation and is also on staff at the Stephen J. Ruggiero Funeral Home, Pen Argyl, PA. Romond lives in Wind Gap, PA with his wife, Mary, their son, Liam, and their Bichon Frise, Oscar.

CPSIA information can be obtained
at www.ICGtesting.com
Printed in the USA
BVHW041756200521
607798BV00002B/368